the pearl is a
hardened sinner

notes from kindergarten

the pearl is a hardened sinner

notes from kindergarten

by STANLEY KIESEL

with a foreword by
CARL RAKOSI

Nodin Press, Minneapolis

For Harold Kittleson
Best Wishes!
Stanley Kiesel
May 9, 198,

Some of these poems have appeared in the
following: *Antioch Review, Coastlines,
Contact, Minnesota Poets Anthology — 1973,
The New Voices, Studio One* and
25 Minnesota Poets.

Cover design by David Lunn

Four new poems have been added
to the original Scribner's edition;
*Grade Five, Principal,
Sixth Grade* and *Arnold.*

Nodin Press, Inc.
519 North Third St., Minneapolis, MN 55401
Printed in U.S.A. at
Harrison, Smith - Lund Press, Minneapolis

for Polly and Emily

contents

foreword

This book, an enlargement of one published by
Scribner's in 1968, subtitled *Notes from Kindergarten,*
belongs with the special delights of anchovies,
Greek olives, salami & eggs, and the cartoonist William
Steig's *Small Fry.* I can not make up my mind
whether its extraordinary flavor is due to the fact that
Mr. Kiesel's small fry are too deprived and real to be
cute, their situations too miserable for sentimental
emotions, or whether it's due to his extraordinary
self-discipline in excluding all trace of the sentimental
and the cute in order to keep a solid hold on reality
and his teaching function intact, and, I suspect, protect
himself against too deep a personal involvement.
Perhaps it's due to a little of both and to the fact that
that function requires distance and understanding
and humor . . . of which this book is full . . . and is never
sentimental or cute.

In any case, these poems are a triumph over
the classroom experience. They are a triumph of
feeling, bitter-sweet as it really is, and peasant realism,
as when he writes of Ronnie, "the cardiac boy . . . on
relief since he was born":

"Ears, nose, throat;
Doctor squints at him like a bag of nails."

And in the same vein, a triumph of metaphors, the
most extraordinary metaphors, delightful, zany
surprises, as when he calls Marsha, "You little
unaddressed envelope." And a triumph of humor,
extraordinary for its empathy: John, for instance:

"I remember you too . . . whose feigned deafness
Was all you had your mother could not bathe;
Your private mafia was the pants you filled from
    day to day."

And wit:

"When called upon, an expression
Crawls into his eyes as if he were
Suddenly afraid I was going to introduce
Him to himself in too large a dose."

I could quote on and on. You can see that I can't
get these little shavers out of my mind.

CARL RAKOSI

ix

I

marsha

To everything she has a hunchbacked response.
She looks like something spoiled in the darkroom;
She inhabits dresses rather than wears them.

Seven times today she washed her hands.
She embarrasses the blackboards.

Mother arrives, parachuting in from the society
    page.
Her soup kitchens, she proclaims, are at our
    disposal;
But the charity closest to her heart (she insists)
    is her pet child.

You alms-giver, there is nothing non-profit about
    you,
Your breasts are selfish with milk.
This child was a hobby of your bedclothes,
A little memorial to an expensive perfume.

—Go, go wash your hands, Marsha!
You little unaddressed envelope.

ronnie

The scale is erect and as prim as a spinster;
The eye-chart too, has a no-nonsense look about
   it.
Here, both doctor and nurse sit it out,
Both starched, and chewing unsweetened gum.

Enter: "the cardiac boy":
There's a rigid fist inside him
That knocks out the windows of rest,
Gives him the black eyes of an insomniac.

Ears, nose, throat;
Doctor squints at him like a bag of nails.

Helpless mother is a pincushion, mewing in our
   face;
Father: a shellacked cigar with punched-out eyes;

And the social worker is one of those intellectuals
Who sicks her knowledge on you like a dog.

Neglected, on relief since he was born,
He is the test tube of our school.
In a moment of reckless grace we let him in.
To thank us he flushed all our toilets.

Not a day passes that he does not ascend in that
     fiery balloon
To empty himself on our heads.

Our love is his receptacle.

seven children

David's eyes held his mind's reins so no
    thought stampeded.
Michael Dean gave his urine to secret agents
    and never washed his hands.
Virginia was alone among us all, the baggage
    car of her mother's care.
And Johanna was a sea that never conferred
    with anyone.

Where are you now, children? Rendered visible,
    I expect;
Wearing tight shoes, run over by a hundred
    trucks;
Terrifyingly suspect of planting aphis on your
    parents' roses.

Albert, you leaped off conversation's cliff
    and never did come back,
Whereas you, Lynn, were the overtrained athlete
    of your mother's tongue.
And John—I remember you too—whose feigned
    deafness
Was all you had your mother could not bathe;
Your private mafia was the pants you filled
    from day to day . . .

To the mass-produced adult all children look
    homemade.

And so they are, who have not yet learned to do
    anything on credit:
The world is whatever they pick up off the
    ground.
We, who swallow our duties like medicine,
Our salutes are always on time.

April, fifty-six. Children, the future's good
    if you endure.
Do not shave off those sweet mustaches.

casey

The paintbrush leaps like a fishing pole
Landing Black, Orange, Green, goggle-eyed
And wriggling on paper. She works, wearing
Her mouth's tight shoes, her eyes sawing
Distances in half. The temper that makes her
A cannibal of the playyard, on paper emerges
Like a sound piece of non-fiction.

Not one jot of your gift do they guess:
Your mother, father, so buried in a snow
Of money and money-cares; her talent lies
In stocking up canned goods, and his, in
Breastfeeding his lawn. I've met them;
They look as if their pleasure has had a flat
          tire.

Tie a can to the world's tail, Casey, and take
This advice: art is presumption, so saddle it.
Intellect, before it became a cut flower
Belonged to a bush, trust insight
To be your body's best fisherman.
Your muscular tongue, untidy laughter,
Won't win you friends
But color will never disapprove of you.
Bite into the green certainty then spit
And never say thank you.

danny

The first day, wheeled to my room
In a little red wagon. His tibia,
As well as his confidence, broken.

"Say hello to your teacher, Danny."

The overblown head blinks its bald
Eyes. Mother, like a golfstick,
Has smacked his presence so hard
That he falls into the rough and is lost.

"We just came to be introduced.
The Doctor says Danny has to stay
At home for at least six weeks."

The other mothers pretend not to listen,
Tact flapping in the wind like flags.
The room is now a leaking boat,
The women row, in juries, out.

And in six weeks he returns,
Lowering his unforgettable presence
Like an anchor into the rug.
He sits. The story, the dramatic play,
Pass over him like clouds. He sits.
When called upon, an expression
Crawls into his eyes as if he were
Suddenly afraid I was going to introduce
Him to himself in too large a dose.

19

"Danny." The pupil jerks in his eye
Like a fish. "Danny." His lips retract.

In the yard he walks—to no one—
Carrying himself like a heavy suitcase.
Or tilting his chin, he stands, staring
At the last boat of himself steaming out the harbor.

grade five

1.

Eternity is property
to Mr. Blank;
a heavenly escrow
where prayers
fly like angels
with wings of
enriched, white bread.

This pedagogue himself
was once a child,
planted in a pot
and over-watered
by a churchy mother.
All his ideas
still celebrate
the ancient birthday
of his apprehension
by Jesus.
(The smart-alecky kids
groan; the worst movies
are made by God.)

2.

The problem is
not prayers in school,

21

or putting Our Lord
in the flag salute,
but whether pity
is born warm-blooded
and natural.

3.

Real religion
holds its tongue;
wants its privacy;
is noways careful;

cannot be
copyrighted

and never
acts the bellboy,

carrying our bags
in and out
of Sunday.

II

gregg

Gregg, you cork, speck of a great saint,
I wish all your exits well.

The world's cold entertainment without you.
Never a detractor or an amuser,

But a solid occupant of the actual,
What you gave me never graced your mind.

Modesty was your grandfather.
If indeed, you were a child,

You were better than all the candy offered me,
Better than the apples, because Gregg,

You were the bite itself.

A child like you is a clearing,
The era's arable land;

Such a man that even your failures
Will find employment.

Gregg, there's no paper pleasure
Worth the thing you are.

kim

Horses and dogs call for caresses, not
You, Kim. You were a fact, you never took
Graft. I see you, nagging the gravel
With your feet . . . Did you keep the pebbles
In hopes that they would mother you?

Each kid rides his own range, makes
A snowball of our advice to
Throw at us. Eyes like a scissors,
This boy will always desert his
Teachers and everyone else, because
He's one of many making no covenant
With anyone, tête-à-tête only with his thumb.

No one ever found out who had made him.
For years we gave him old clothes and shots,
Airdropping down to him the powdered
Milk of our pity . . . Sometimes, knowledge is a
Suitcase we pack too late. Kim, you melted
Away out of sight, and we were left
With a file, an aging parenthesis
Clasping the souvenirs of our good intentions.

reflection at noon

The ill, rebelliously ill children, remind me
Of men out of work; and so they are: out of play.
They live their childhood under assumed names.
Tommy, whose glance was a stick, we never won;
And Mary Louise, whose very breathing seemed
Bandaged: lost to us; scores of kids hauling
Around their miseries in little jinrikshas.

How can we heal,
Becalmed on our blunders,
Measuring ourselves
With rulers,
Ejaculating our
Own abstinence?

Resolutions give us
Boils. Candor brings
On cramps. We castrate
Our bodies and give
Genitalia to our
Illusions. Is there
An absurdity we
Haven't made love to?

The reprehensible parent is everywhere:
In Washington, cleaning his chlorophyll bomb
(Parent as politician; politician as mortician);
As the Administrative Insecta of our public schools
Or one of those lumpen intellectuals in the

Universities (poverty of tense and of mode);
Serving in the diabetic church or among the
Sugarless police; as that hemorrhage of our
Public lives, the Adman, selling us his well-
Boxed anal prowess; or as one of a dozen hystericals
Thumping the boards for the glad war or the
Sad peace. All over the world, neurosis, taking
    us into custody.

With a face like a doily,
Jane's mother looked as if
All her experiences had worn
Galoshes; her aim was not
To conceive but to stock-pile
Her children. And her husband—
His love was a hastily bought
Ticket, his good intentions
Always last in line.

We have dollars but none of us has sails.
We either suffer from engine failure,
Have forced landings, or become the branded
Animals of political cannibals. We devour
Our children then expect to regurgitate them
    whole.

We fathers are 'lower-case': the after-dinner
Speakers, the family matadors; AWOL with
Our poker hands, or off having affairs
With our new cars. We mothers are in 'caps':
The M.C.'s of our youngsters' bowels,
Charging hysterectomies to our credit cards;
The local piranha of the P.T.A..

With what are we rewarding ourselves: coarse
Durable uniforms and dislocated bones? The
Intellectually jobless? Brainless salvation?
    Easily-ignited
Deductions and dead-drunk devotions? The
    piddling
Unriddled existence that always says, *please*?

della

Wearing a little false beard
Of ill-will and a toxic grin,
She rides hard the broomstick
Of her mother's defection.

With relish, relates such slivers
Of news as dogs being hit,
Babies breaking their legs,
Planes colliding with trains.
With her it's always Halloween.

How can we love her,
She can only be taken intravenously.

III

teresa

So terrifying
Is her
Piety
That on
Her pronouncement
Of "grace"
The custard
Runs

She transforms
The class
Into a choir
Singing
Mary Had a Little Lamb

I find her
Bitten fingernails
All over the rug
In the shapes
Of little crosses

You can tell
How old she is
By counting the rings
Around her eyes

Sitting at the
Bottom
Of a wastebasket

33

Fragments
Of a disposable world
Fall on her head

—God   where did you hide her
Jump rope

miss r.

Her bun, the spinster's monument,
Low on her neck.
Eyes: an unblinking brown,
But bare, like two worn slippers;
Nose: a long and porous objection
To the tyranny of an immodest mustache;
And a small and sensual mouth,
With not a trace on its lips
Of the lonely rooms it has devoured.
Her tall figure striding like a man's,
Raises a flag of gratitude
In each mother's eye,
Because she is the undisputed sovereign
Of their bully-boys,
So strong she rides them side-saddle.
The classroom proclaims her didactic prowess.
The children bear the stigmata
Of printed matter on their foreheads;
Their brains are black and blue
With homage to Dickens, Van Gogh,
And the brackish fragments of Melville.
Miss R.'s voice is always in italics
—Even as she whispers her voice kicks.
Her large hands promise to knock children
Into the conscious salvation of Calculus-Made-
    Easy
And Idiomatic Russian.
When she is inspired distances are emptied
Of their horizons,

And she distributes roads.
For those children who have somewhere to go
She is their rucksack,
Overflowing with emergency provisions.

Once in a decade there comes a boy
Possessing the quality of being at
Right angles to the world;
In whose eyes plays the imperishable music
Of real ideas.
The day Ted first took his seat
She saw his mind soar up from its eyrie
Like an eagle, and succumbed.
Henceforth her dreams were Columbus-ridden
And she was robbed of rest.
He was bright but he needed leonine aims,
Her provocative regime for his irascible desires.
And the familiar ache burst in her bosom.
The hairy face of his father
Had frozen over, and the sentiment
His mother showed him
Seemed void of significance.
Family living was a dumb-show performance
Of rigid antics and unforgivable attentions.
He was like a bucket
Knocking against the sides of a well,
With no ready hand to pull him up.
And then the tall bony woman
Who looked like a female signor,
Chatting over a cup of dislike
With his mother, revealed to herself
She would train him for greatness.
Suddenly, the sunlight was all male,
And she basked in it.

Became as playful as a porpoise;
The active sweetness rose
From the games of the playyard
To permeate her pores,
And she laughed like a teen-age charlatan.

Her sense of faith was acute.
Arriving at seven,
She set up her room as a lover would.
Art prints, language records,
Materials of science, they each
Lay like relics of saints, open for homage;
All the skills of the past thirty years
Gathered as if at a convention.
At eight, he entered: the books
Opened their mouths and sang.
They looked at Cezanne,
Dug deep into Emily's iron-hearted fancies,
And undermined the school
With the Red Army Chorus.
He breathed with awe,
As if he'd been let in a mansion.
Though her lessons were dressed
In stern clothes, what she concealed
Wore a big hat, and he saw it,
And grew larger.
But at nine, when the others trouped in,
She changed;
It was like his visa had given out;
She seemed to stop breathing,
Only her eyes inhaled,
And he lost his footing;
Stumbled against the hardness in her
And fell, and was not helped up.

She was compelled to be harsh,
So much giving weakened her
—Until the next day,
When with her seven o'clock key,
She opened herself up again.
For weeks and months she spoon-fed him
The genius of the past,
Pounded as on an anvil
Shoeing his sensibility;
And feeding him, she nourished herself.
Now at night there was no longer time
For her old violin,
Stashed in its case near her antique fur,
Nor for solitaire,
Or the television she drank from
Like a bottle;
Engrossed as she was,
Proofreading her passion;
Transmuting its higher mathematics.

Her mood was unmistakable
And gossip spread like branches
Down a stream;
The men guffawed, the women shook their heads.
She became the inmate of every joke,
The resident of whispers,
The denizen of that jungle
We all, at one time, go headhunting in.
But the boy grew;
His once clumsy mind learned to dance,
But like those ethereal puffs of grace
That display at firsthand
A sizable calf,
His thinking was tough.

What Miss R. made him feel
Was that he was an heir to an estate,
And that the crucial part
Of his inheritance was himself.
He thought of her
As some divine giantess of nonidentity,
In the boughs of an enormous tree
Handing him apples,
Which somehow grew arms and cradled him.
He could intuit
That she was someone
A drowning man might grasp
To save himself, and being saved, discard;
And with unconscious cruelty
He grew more tender than he should,
And in her friendless room at night
The violin shuddered with misgivings.

Memories of other boys
Sighed through her like the wind:
Harvey, in thirty-four;
Dennis, in forty-six; and Ralph,
Irrepressible Ralph,
Whose grin had rolled under a wheel in . . .
She did not want to remember.
That this relationship
Was a tinderbox in which she would be
Reduced to ashes—as in the past—
She knew, but turned her back;
There was the present and her task.
Old age yawned at her from the mirror;
Impending retirement
Burned like a coal in her bosom.
Children had always stolen from her;

They sensed her devotion
And pressed it into service.
Now, at the end of her career,
She felt defrauded.
The workpapers she took home to correct
Stared at her like blueprints of deception.
The boy would graduate
And she would pocket—what?
A soft goodbye?
The visitations that would gutter
Like a candle—and then go out?

But the intrepid hope
That she had been part of someone
Sustained her.
And so the semester closed.
And when the last farewell
Escaped her door
She emptied desk and cleaned her blackboard
And robbed the vases of their flowers;
Martial law ruled her eye.
That night
There were solemn lakes in the sky.
Listening, the old violin
Heard the black clouds roll and break.
The spouts began to beat their drums . . .
And from the lawns
The cloud burst brought the gophers up
And escorted them brusquely down the gutters.
And if—or when—
The old maid launched her misery,
Who might know?
No one had ever heard.

Over the soiled rags of the sky
Sailed the tuneless flotilla of the rain.

belinda

This five year old burglar
Has stolen me out of myself.
Without socks and in an
Emaciated dress, she
Twitters and warbles and
Whistles and pokes the
Sun in the ribs.
This culturally-deprived
Mexican child dances
Upon nothing. Fortunately,
Joy has no need of soap
Or water—nor a ribbon
In its hair (children
Are its ribbons), it needs
Only the indestructible
Assent. And Belinda,
Little cicada, sings
Without any operatic
Ambitions. Life would
Not be worthwhile
If one could not throw
Snowballs at the Mona Lisa.

IV

principal

Her girdle
And *Robert's*
Rules of Order
Pull her together.

Indefatigable
Bootblack
Of trivia,
Today she
Cannot see
Anyone; she is
Giving birth
To paper clips.

Yesterday,
When we suggested
She give
The troubled kids
A room
To vent their
Troubles in,
A checkerboard
To crown their
Disappointments on,
And someone (myself)
To win from,
Without reprisal,
She nixed it,
Saying: it's not
Our responsibility.

Now, let's take A.,
I said. He needs
A playground
To explode in,
And I've got one
Readymade
From three to five.
Then there's B.,
With hammers
For hands.
I'd give him nails
Instead of spelling,
Syllables of wood
To smooth, slivers
For homework . . .
And C., of the
Over-refined family,
She'd be happy
With nothing more
For Christmas
Than dirty hands.

No, she said.
No.
(In her mind,
Each child
Comes to school
Covered by a
Two year warranty
On parts and labor.)

No, she said.
No.
(This kind of
Bureaucrat
Is, in effect,
A Bluebeard:
She marries her job
And then proceeds
To murder it.)
No, she said.
No.

Later, I pass
Her office;
She is vasing
Roses. A confiscated
Marble moons
On her desk.

among the tracts

Here, on all fours among their thoughts,
Play the children. One rolls a ball;
One, in the paddy wagon of his brother's
     arms,
Scowls; one leaves her urine on the lawn
For dogs to sniff; one, with crowds of
     ailments
Perched on his eyebrows, sucks his thumb,
     listens to it purr.

A treasury of the poorly-made litter
     the walks:
Games, toys and trikes; by evening
     forgotten,
Sluffed off on the grass by children
Who have been bailed out of every
     concern,
Whose only terror is orthodontia
Or that their television might suddenly
     drop dead.
And while they sleep, what kind Brownies
Repark their rusting bikes, pick up
     their talking dolls,
Collect their guns, the rubber darts
Of their law-abiding bull's-eyes?

What is this great runny nose
     of houses?

These streets, with their stenciled
        addresses on the curbs,
Baby-sit the kids, never allow them
        to forget
Behind what card they are filed
        at bedtime.

The lawn is laid out like an
        antimacassar
To hide the dirty ground;
And on the roof, the TV repairman
Stands like the Statue of Liberty.

joan

It is because she has already
Volunteered her consent
That this child
Delights in refusals.
A hornless rhinoceros,
She wants me to wince
When I pat her on the head.

Behind my back, a scowl
Falls out of the open pages
Of her face, like a superfluous
Bookmark.

gregory

Your foster mother's dead, goodbye, Gregory;
It's Christmas and you belong to the State.

For what are you looking so sad-eyed?
They have a tree there for you,
Trained staff and a fake Santa.

If horses had portfolios they would study you.
If books had lips they would probably bite you.
A monstrous little future is pasted on your
        forehead.

The matron, who brings you the last day, is a
        cheerleader,
But her affection is full of artificial preservatives;
The natural goodness is gone.
There remains only myself, a stage direction of
        this fraudulent school
Which, like a bank, closes at three.

Au revoir, Gregory, looking like a blank between
        teeth.
—Why the sobs?
I was only guaranteed for one year;
Read the fine print in your contract.

parent conference

Belligerent paint (emotionally disturbed) pours
      Jimmy on its hands;
Attention-getting sand (it has a low I.Q.) rubs
      Jimmy in its hair;
Pitiful clay (obviously retarded) chews Jimmy
      in its mouth;
Nothing, no, there is nothing that isn't found
      wanting
(With the exception of Jimmy) by Surrealist
      mother.

Has there ever existed a boy so downright handy
At flooding sinks? Or such a crackshot where
Collisions are concerned? Or with such a gift
      for amnesia?

This little beachcomber of the sandbox,
This bizarre little gourmet of his nose,
I can visualize him now, signing Bills
With one shoe off and one shoe on;
Blowing his straw paper at the French
      Ambassador;
Spilling his milk at the Summit.
The Republicans will most assuredly get him.

Yet, this Phi Beta Kappa of mishaps,
What a purveyor of joy: packs a grin like a gun;
A humor that says: experience is no palace;
Perfection can only be made from chemicals

52

And we are all naturalised citizens of someone
    else's conceptions . . .
Well, if the Presidency is never his—
Or anything else—what matter?
The world will treat our casualty lightly
And forgive the breakage.

sonya

Her black bangs are better for her than any
    cereal;
Exquisitely frame the independent votes
    of her eyes.
Teacher must climb a stepladder to her answer
And only then to find a horse of delicious
    anticipation.
Sonya, your tongue frequents a grassy meadow.
Unique child, this ball's a superfluity;
You laugh in your throat as you throw it to me.

v

sisters

Laura: homely, silent; tattooed by her mother's
High voice lying in ambush for her;
Anne: a trophy of intercourse, pretty,
With large audible eyes and a backyard
Teeming with personnel. One: eaten into
By moths, the other: a chocolate-covered son.

Anne could scramble up that greased pole
Of her father's criterion like a monkey,
Whereas Laura failed over and over,
Could not even chin herself on the bar
Of a simple command. Full of the pins
Of good sense, both children were the able
Manikins of their parents' mania for
Self-sufficiency; large economy-size packages
Of reading and writing; two little drudges
In the forced-labor camp of their father's
        workbooks.

Eventually, Anne was double-promoted
While Laura was borne on the back of a siren
Past my room, past the horizon.
She died—unlike anything she had done in life—
With ease.
And all that remained were her A.B.C.'s,
Meandering like a painful train of crippled ants
Across her notebook.

sammy

From an old coffee can,
A quarantined cricket
Is playing a concerto.

Large symphonic works,
In the shape of blades of grass,
Issue from a shoebox.

Stones and stamps and cat's eye marbles;
Sammy dreams, adrift,
In a sea of assemblage.

A lonely boy in a crowd of bottlecaps.

The children who relate only to animals
Or the inanimate,
They haul up their compliance
And cast off.

They do not speak—or if they do,
Their conversations are cross-eyed.
Anxiety is a mosquito
And they are full of bites.

It is you, Sammy,
In the jar with the clamped-down lid,
Wrestling with quiet.

bob and lance

Bob, toothless and shy, his eyes
Stringing a needle; Lance, listening
To no one but his friend's impaired
Speech. Arms entwined, they'd hike
Through every response, riding the
Rails of their own jokes.

The world's an old horror movie,
Boys, where you'll pay for every
Inch to be yourself. The ne'er-do-wells
Who pray on credit, the jinglers
Who don inhibition's cap and bells,
The anteaters whose offers have pimples
On them, in times to come will all
Be your teachers. Learn from them.

Recall this affection when you are
Old and most humane. And be proud.
It was love that made you good.
And as for brotherhood, tell Man,
Bob and Lance, what he must do:
Be his own highest bidder.

perry

His mouth : cloth;
Speech sewn

　　　　　to the top
　　　　　of his voice.

That inflexible jaw
And self-made exit
Made me lonely;

　　　　it said :

　　　　　　a grin
　　　　　　is a way
　　　　　　of escape;

　　　　　　I am
　　　　　　my own
　　　　　　Punch and Judy.

Perry,
Child of rags and wood,
You grasped my puppet's
Hand so hard

It pinched me
Into insight :

　　　　　　"I love and ⁻
　　　　　　will abuse
　　　　　　each child
　　　　　　who is
　　　　　　my caricature."

sixth grade

1.

Nice observers
of their brainy neighbors,

rightful owners
of wrong answers,

ambiguous authors
of homely fanfares,

grievances
hang from their lips
like stalactites.

2.

Trigger finger
cocked on her grade book,
the times tables
surrender,
arms in the air.

Whoever picked
her sex's pocket
was never forgiven.

3.

World's war surely
is on love.

It is when we pray
the hardest

that someone's feet
are sticking out our mouths.

4.

When I see how
the young must live,
rounding themselves off
to the nearest
decimal point,

I am convinced
it is only
children
who bear
the credentials

to untie our way of life
like a shoelace

and throw it away.

the divine average

There was Mark, whose vision weighed a ton,
Becalmed on his two buck teeth;
And David of the right-angled ears;

And Judy, whose love for me announced
To all other children Standing Room Only;
And Bill, polite retcher, baritone of the

Wastebasket. Dressed in tongue-tied perfection:
Peggy, and Greta, a whiner, with a voice like
A forceps. Fifty-odd Lindas and eighty-one

Bobs; wet pants and hiccoughs;
Hundreds of miles of slightly crossed eyes.

These children will hitch a ride with anything
I say, burglarizing my words, my looks, my laugh,
Even my pretense at being stern. . . And that is

Just. Because in a sense, they are wet-nursing
Their future history. They have names,
They are in the custody of their nature.

They shall vote, give homage to and vase
Their opinions, yes and chase indiscretion
With hounds; because they are in sequence.

Salud, all my Bobs and Davids, Kathys
And Lindas, you are that extensible filament
Wound upon the firmament. Demand nothing

But your own direction; thread the deity.

VI

doris

Eyes filled with underweight
Expressions, and a pin in her voice.
Discovered her in my class
One day, stuck, like a piece of
Gum, to the bottom of my shoe.

She, one of too many children
I know, so politely mangled it
Makes me mournful to teach;
Sexless, glassy, a tuneless little
Sample for the kodak ("say cheese"),
Retiring more and more into her
Skin eruptions. Today, sent to me
In a peacock dress, she will not
Paint but remains crouched in
A corner, crushed, like a pack animal,
Beneath a mother's ribbon.

larry

This pampered darling of his lunch pail
(His sandwiches need a truss),
Is the matinee idol
Of every hippopotamus.
Whales have crushes on him.

One look at him and basketballs
Lose their illusions.

What happens to the childhood
He pretends to play with?
Is it stored up for the winter,
For the long adult sleep?

Above his shadow, his thoughts fly South,
Where the girls he is afraid of talk to him,
And the boys proffer rides on their bikes . . .

What will become of him
In a world lighter-than-air?

one family

Diana, eleven, is the oldest; she dances
While all the time her mind is knitting;
Behind her face is a measure; she looks at you
And her eyes are writing like pencils.

Harry's wide open; no part of him that isn't let
        for rent.
For the promulgation of laughter
He has established a princely grin.
Yet, hovering over his lips, like a tiny moth,
Is the solemnity of an unseen mustache
That bristles like Moses to make seas open.

Cecilia is the kind of child who could barrel
        down Niagara
In round numbers. Her head is full of setting
        hens.
In that concise and sober suitcase she carries
        off to camp
There is nothing that hasn't been sworn into
        office.
Her puppets are all in their right minds.

Richard's logic has a hairy chest
And he bares it. He has no need of a teacher,
His questions water their own lawn.
Wherever his thoughts travel to, God only knows,
But they go on foot.

Here are parents who are not concerned over the
    digestibility of their opinions;
Whose home is without those toileted virtues
That have become so crucial to our culture,
Those certificated permissions to breathe in and
    breathe out.

These humans have vertebrae.
They possess the viscera of individuality.
Their lives have not been quarantined by
    television.
Nor do they fly their credit cards on Lincoln's
    Birthday.
You look upon them gravely sewing buttons on
Their identity and you know that because of them
A spirit exists in the world that is vertical.

arnold

Stands outside the sandbox
like a U.N. observer.

He enlightens his older sister,
his cleaning lady,
the gardener and
pediatrician.
Is never sleepy,
reports Mother,
only bored.

How proud she is
of being her son's equal.
Both parents
keep Arnold well-armed
with the latest
educational toy.

"One hundred sixty,"
she tells me,
as we watch Arnold float
in the sea of children,
holding on to his high I.Q.
like a life preserver.

postgraduate

From the foxholes of status I pursue my degree,
This prescription-for-glasses learning.
My small strummers and drummers
Know more than these hairless memorials
Sucking at their stale anthologies' pieces of candy.
These profs are no match for the octopus-armed
    devotion,
The vision openly-prayed-for, of my children,
Who are better teachers and are never drunk on
    submission.
Kindergarten by day, at dusk, the University;
From the delirious surplus to the prissy donation.

The professors recline in the easy chairs of their
Minds, cavalierly distributing their ideas
Like so many urine specimens to impoverished
Lab technicians. The air is ponderous with
Their overly-masticated words and dessicated
Thoughts. The hours spent with them drag
Like barnacled anchors along a sea bottom.

How can anyone find the scent here among
These morticians and confidence-men? There
Is a diploma here for everything—except thought.
Principles, Curriculum, and Developmental
    Methods;
Psychological and Sociological Foundations;
Elementary Arts and Secondary Crafts;
Speech Problems and Human Geography;

The History of Aural Rehabilitation
For the Prematurely Blind—everything for
The training teacher but his subject:
The child.

There is little use in prostrating ourselves
    before textbooks,
We are the texts. What has Education to do
    with these
Anthills; with these hewers of wood and drawers
    of water? Mouths open and close,
We are infected only by our professor's colds.
To trim possibilities, that is the goal, and
    in so doing,
To become the parochial masseurs of insipid
    certainties. It is a contest
Of contradiction so let us ignore it. Better
    let us sail out
Toward the freakish environs where the answers
    are slim,
Where nothing lies under the Christmas tree but
Ourselves. There we can put to proof the power
Of being men and women in a joyful context;
    moving from the tame room
Into the membership of the air; marrying
    ourselves
Off, so to speak, to the earth. For we must
    remember
That institutions, by nature, tend to be
    murderous:
Say to us: come out with your hands up
—And there we stand, on the cross hair. At least
If we must close up our youth within these four
Walls we call seats of learning, let us cast out

73

The cigarette-burned lecterns and bring in kids
To teach them; educationally 'pack in'; not go off
On safari with our library cards to shoot game
We'll never eat. All these *Advanced Studies*,
　　　Seminars, and *Graduate Projects*
Are just a way of goading bulls to squander
　　　themselves on red flags.—Enough!

Teachers of tomorrow,
You far-reaching, super-excellent
Short order cooks for the common denominator,

Lift up the world's dress and look!

VII

during the summer

As lovely as a drop
Of water, friendly
As ink, a Sunflower,
With the sweetness
Of the bees in her eyes.

This morning, with a bit
Of bread, she sustained
A sparrow, and gave
The horses and cows
Her fingertips, and the
Puppy her thumb to lick.

I pass her on the
Road, a little soloist
Of the fields, escorting
The seasons on their
Enthusiastic rounds;
Her glance, as round
As a wheel; her
Forehead full of ships.

billy

Looking   like a
Chewed   stubby   pencil

With   stick mouth
And   Out To Lunch   eyes

Since   father expects
Only   disasters

He gives him   one   daily
As a   gift

Her smile   reads
Keep   Off   the   Grass

: No passport
To mother

In class
Sits in   fist

Forging   his
Signature

To every
Lost   penny

And   this is
His
Story:

Wetting
And

Awaiting
Arrest

jamie

Snowman of mirth, small hired hand, erase the
    board
But do not ever erase that infectious scribble
    on your face.
It is not important to discover what you celebrate,
The single and lovely animal within you that
    cavorts to make me happy,
The joy in you, Jamie, is a certificate of birth
    for everyone.

joey

Ink, jam, chocolate, what does not pay you its
    respects?
There is not a grain of sand which has not been
    invited into your shoes.
Was a comb ever elected to run through your hair?

Pinching, pulling, prancing, puling,
The whole day is prickled with you.
That small cluster of flexible parts
Which is you, Joey,
Avalanches down on everyone's goodwill.

Funds are dolefully paid out to keep you clean,
To punctuate your warm palms with pennies,
But vengeful and mucid, you spill and shriek,
And welt the water glasses with your greasy thumbs
And buy up even more land with your homeless
    anger.

If this entire school despises you
It is because, poor child,
Your wrath engenders fluids:
You bring on all these old maids' periods.

Lord help us who can do nothing here
But aid and abet you like a crime—
Grafters all of us! (Pity is a
Minor and shall never gain the vote.)
God grant long life to your rages, Joey;
Our bruises belong to you if nothing else.

81

kindergarten teacher

Her intentions are to see that Blue
Is never painted next to Green,
And that the sexes use separate toilets.
Governed by the laws of washbasins, the
Children become little domestics
Of her hysteria.

Her spirit is like a wilderness;
Her face has no water hole. Every
Sham can burp her, any psychopath can
Have her for dessert. If she does love
Something she makes a meal out of it.
A few gray hairs
Are the extent of her ideas.

Today, while the boys and girls
Rest upon their backs, she plans
Her summer trip. Tickets
Take her nowhere.

She belongs to that all-powerful,
International body: The Association
For the Advancement of the Idea
That Intractable Children
Be Given Off As Vapor.

thoughts at dismissal

Down the rapids of three o'clock
The kids shoot home; forgotten,
A miraculous painting reels down
The street. Children do not need
You, you Sunday Sheriffs of the Lord,
They keep a pew in the weather;
The sun is their hat.

To teach—what does it mean?
It means to rise entire; to be
A birthmark; to be surrounded
By shoelaces and vegetarian
Lovemaking; to produce, from a
Milk-mustachioed Beethoven,
An unmistakable thumbprint on music.

Nothing these children say ever
Asks for wages. Their aspirations
Run around on bare feet. Their
Secrets all have diarrhea. And
These have been my ABC's:
Not to laugh as if I were running
For an office; not to be a stickler
Because certainty jilts us; not to
Have a baton or be a cold rifleman.
And as for smugness—when I behave
As if I'd been born in a manger,
The children all carry ear trumpets.
· · · · · · · · · · ·

Lord, first, spare the children
From their parents; from the fools
As well as the pedantic maniacs;
One, bestowing lucrative devotion,
The other, bedridden with ethical
Discouragements.
Second, save them
From their teachers; the swamp-like
Ones, full of submerged refusals,
As well as those busy extending mangy
Invitations, the belligerent virgins.
Third, defend them from their governments;
The decrepit daydreams, the armed
Insistences, the clubfooted concessions
Of politicians.
Lastly, Lord, protect
Them from the war between the rich and
The poor; from a world in heat;
From round-shouldered Science standing at
      attention
Before the bemedaled cripple in the grandstand.

about the author

Stanley Kiesel was born in Los Angeles
where he taught kindergarten for
seventeen years. His poems have
appeared in various magazines and he
has been anthologized. He is married,
with two daughters. Since 1971, he has
been poet in residence for the
Minneapolis Public Schools.